21st Century Junior Library

DISCOVER THE MASTODON

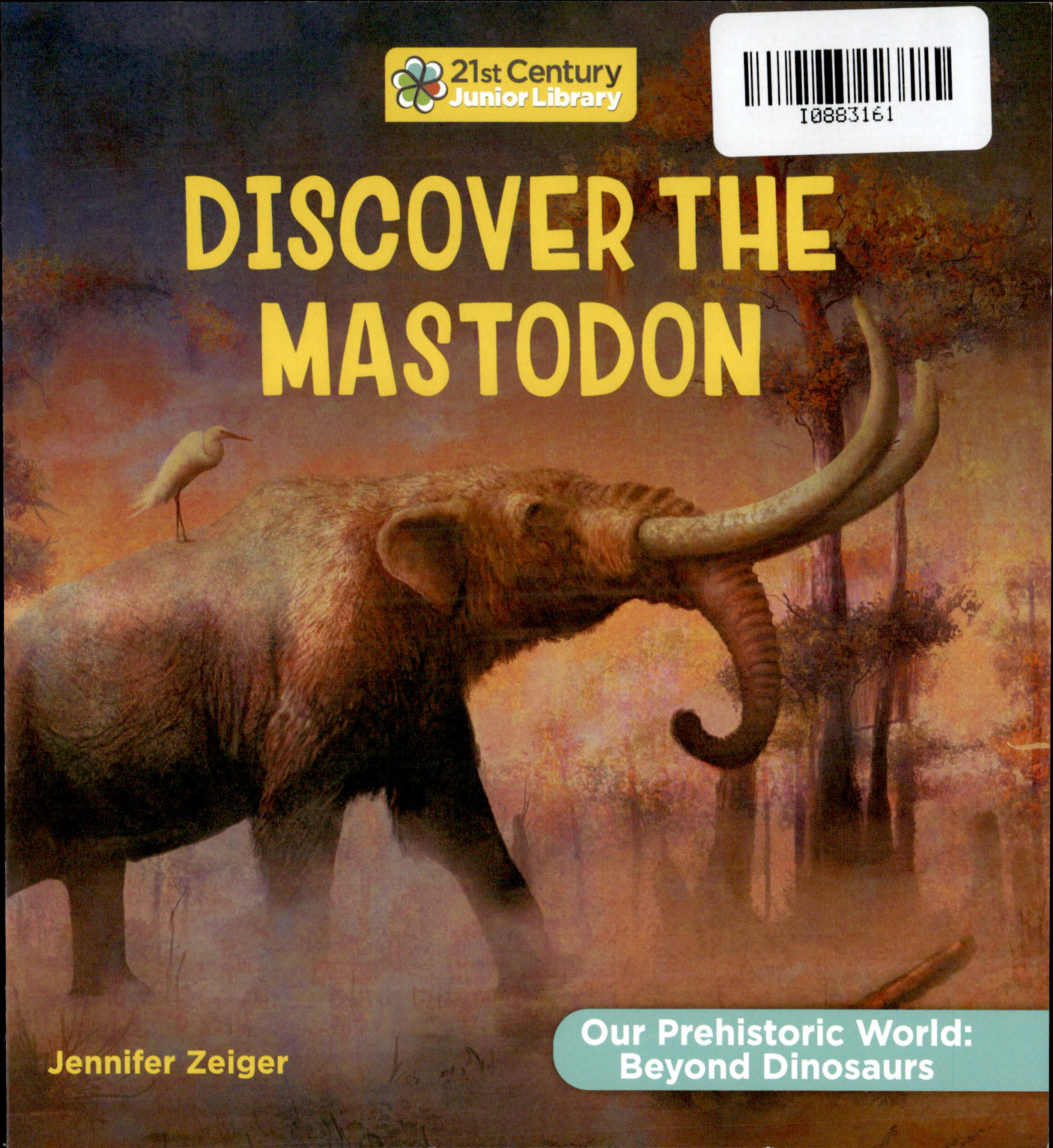

Jennifer Zeiger

Our Prehistoric World: Beyond Dinosaurs

Published in the United States of America by:

CHERRY LAKE PRESS
2395 South Huron Parkway, Suite 200, Ann Arbor, Michigan 48104
www.cherrylakepress.com

Content Adviser: Gregory M. Erickson, PhD, Dinosaur Paleontologist, Department of Biological Science, Florida State University, Tallahassee, Florida

Reading Adviser: Beth Walker Gambro, MS, Ed., Reading Consultant, Yorkville, IL

Photo and Illustration Credits: © Mark Witton, cover, title page; © Charles R. Knight, Public domain, via Wikimedia Commons, 5; © Vladi333/iStock.com, 6; © Mark Witton, 7; © LAURIE O'KEEFE/SCIENCE PHOTO LIBRARY, 8–9; © AKKHARAT JARUSILAWONG/Shutterstock, 10; © Nicole Piepgras/Shutterstock, 11; © Antonyto/Dreamstime.com, 12–13; © Thomas Faull/iStock.com, 14; Dantheman9758, CC BY-SA 3.0 via Wikimedia Commons, 16–17; Smithsonian Institution Archives, 18; © Carlos Duarte/Dreamstime.com, 19; daryl_mitchell from Saskatoon, Saskatchewan, Canada, CC BY-SA 2.0 via Wikimedia Commons, 20

Cherry Lake Press is an imprint of Cherry Lake Publishing Group.

Library of Congress Cataloging-in-Publication Data has been filed and is available at catalog.loc.gov.

Cherry Lake Press would like to acknowledge the work of the Partnership for 21st Century Learning, a Network of Battelle for Kids. Please visit Battelle for Kids online for more information.

Printed in the United States of America

CHERRY LAKE PRESS

CONTENTS

WHAT WAS A MASTODON?

A **prehistoric** elephant lumbers alone through a thick forest. This is a mastodon. This ancient animal was related to the elephant we know today.

Look!

Look at the picture. How is the mastodon like an elephant today? How is it different?

The earliest mastodons lived about 25 million years ago. The **species** existed for millions of years. Early humans even hunted them for a time. No mastodons live today, though. They died out about 10,000 years ago. They are **extinct**.

What do you think made mastodons go extinct?

Think!

Think about what you know about elephants today. How might mastodons have been similar? How might they have been different?

WHAT DID A MASTODON LOOK LIKE?

Mastodons looked like today's elephants. But they also looked a lot like mammoths. Mammoths are another prehistoric animal. They lived at the same time as mastodons. It can be hard to tell them apart.

One difference between mastodons and mammoths: mastodons had flatter heads!

Mastodons were a little shorter than mammoths. But both mammoths and mastodons had large heads and wide, flat ears. They both had very long noses called trunks. Two big teeth called tusks stuck out of their mouths. These animals had large, heavy bodies. Four thick, strong legs supported them.

Mastodon skeleton (back) and mammoth model (front)

Create!

Mastodons were similar in size to today's elephants. Look up pictures of both animals in books or online. Now draw your own mastodon and elephant. Label the ways they are different from each other.

Mastodons had special teeth. Their **molars** had a cone-shaped bump. Mastodon tusks had gentle curves. Some were almost straight. Mastodons had flat, long skulls. They did not have the dome-shaped skulls of today's elephants. Artists who specialize in prehistoric creatures debate whether or not mastodons had bodies covered in fur.

Make a Guess!

Mastodon tusks are actually teeth! What do you think they could have used them for? Keep reading to see if your guess is right.

This 1898 drawing records that this mastodon tooth weighed 17 pounds (7.7 kilograms).

Mastodon restored.

1, Molar tooth, weighing 17 lbs. 2, Skull of Mastodon of Miocene period.

HOW DID A MASTODON LIVE?

Mastodons lived across North America and Central America. They were also found in Asia, Europe, and Africa. Mastodons lived mostly in forests. In these **habitats**, mastodons ate trees and shrubs. A mastodon's cone-shaped teeth could cut and chew tough twigs and leaves. Its tusks could also scrape off bark to eat.

Herds of mastodons were made up of females and their young. When males grew up, they likely left the herd. They may have lived on their own. They fought other males.

Scientists say male mastodons could be aggressive. They used their tusks and large size to fight other males.

This 1915 image shows a mastodon skeleton in the United States National Museum Natural History Building.

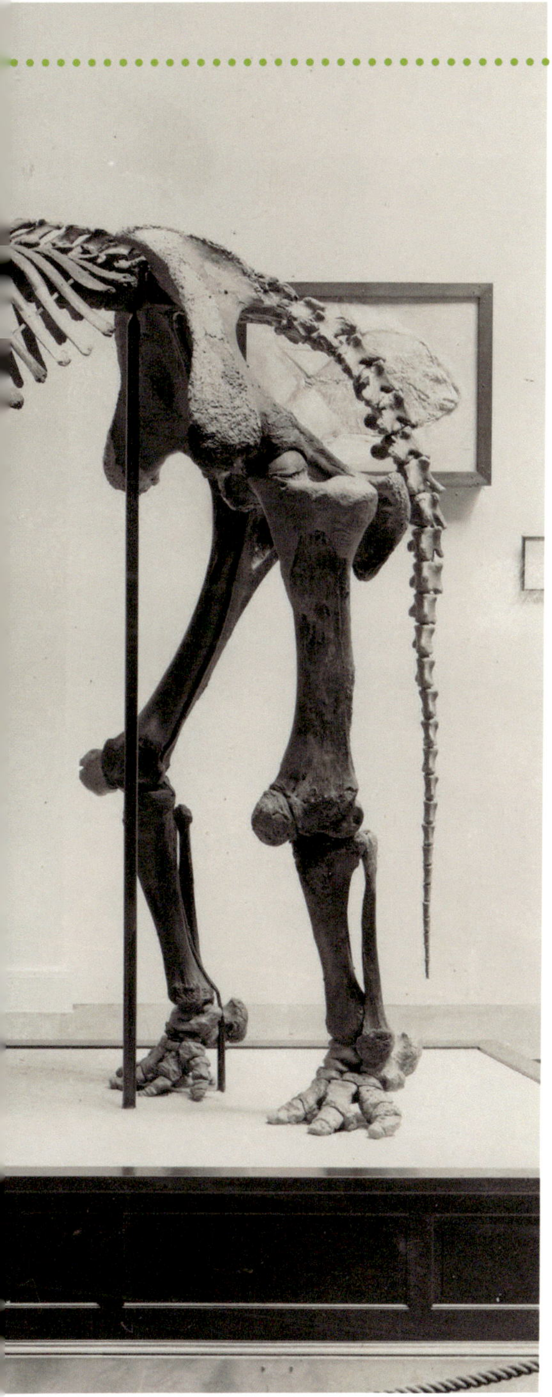

We learn about mastodons in many ways. One way is from **fossils**. Mastodon fossils have been found all over the world.

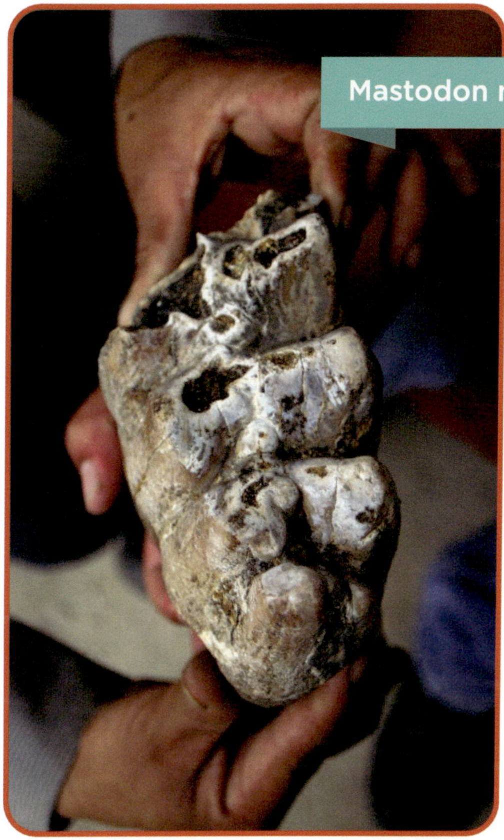

Mastodon molar

These mastodon skeletons were found in the La Brea Tar Pits in Los Angeles, California.

In 2024, a man in New York found some mastodon fossils while mowing his lawn! But we still do not know everything. There is always more to learn about these ancient animals!

Ask Questions!

What else do you want to know about mastodons? Ask a teacher or librarian to help you find answers to your questions. Share what you find out with friends or family.

GLOSSARY

extinct **(ik-STINKT)** no longer found living anywhere on Earth

fossils **(FAH-suhlz)** remains or traces of plants, animals, and other living things that have been preserved as rocks

habitats **(HAA-buh-tats)** places where a plant or animal normally lives

herds **(HURDZ)** large groups of animals that stay or move together

molars **(MOH-luhrz)** back teeth in mammals that are used for grinding

prehistoric **(pree-hih-STOR-ik)** belonging to a time before history was recorded in written form

species **(SPEE-sheez)** group of living things that share many characteristics and can mate and produce offspring

FIND OUT MORE

Books

Dooley, Dr. Brett S., and Krystle Drouault. *A Fossil Journey: The Story of the Pacific Mastodon.* Hemet, CA: Western Science Center, 2020.

Lopetz, Christian. *Rise of the Giant Mammals.* Ann Arbor, MI: Cherry Lake Press, 2026.

Murray, Julie. *American Mastodon.* Minneapolis, MN: ABDO, 2024.

Websites

With an adult, learn more online with these suggested searches.

The Field Museum: Mammoths and Mastodons | Titans of the Ice Age
Check out images of these ancient animals and learn about a baby mammoth that was discovered in the ice of Siberia.

Science Journal for Kids: What can tusks tell us about the lives of mastodons?
Read about mastodon tusks, how they grow, and what we can learn from them.

INDEX

ABOUT THE AUTHOR

Jennifer Zeiger lives in Chicago, Illinois. She writes and edits children's books on all sorts of topics.

About Paleoartists

Paleoartists bring the prehistoric world to life! They work with scientists, paleontologists, museums, and their own research to recreate living things from long, long ago. **Mark Witton** is one paleoartist featured in this series. He has been studying prehistoric creatures for over 20 years! **Brian Engh** is another. He builds sculptures, too. He designs and builds whole exhibits. He started Living Relic Productions.